Miss Lady Bird's Wildflowers
Text copyright © 2005 by Kathi Appelt
Illustrations copyright © 2005 by Joy Fisher Hein
Manufactured in China by South China Printing Company Ltd.
www.harperchildrens.com

Library of Congress Cataloging-in-Publication Data
Appelt, Kathi, date.
Miss Lady Bird's wildflowers : how a First Lady changed America / by Kathi Appelt ;
illustrated by Joy Fisher Hein. — 1st ed.   p.   cm.
Summary: A biography of Lady Bird Johnson, who, as the wife of President Lyndon Johnson,
reminded citizens about the importance of conserving natural resources and promoted the
beautification of cities and highways by planting wildflowers.
ISBN 0-06-001107-6 — ISBN 0-06-001108-4 (lib. bdg.)
1. Johnson, Lady Bird, 1912- — Juvenile literature. 2. Presidents' spouses — United States — Biography —
Juvenile literature. 3. Environmental protection—United States—History —
20th century — Juvenile literature. 4. Roadside improvement — United States — History —
20th century — Juvenile literature. 5. Urban beautification — United States — History —
20th century — Juvenile literature. [1. Johnson, Lady Bird, 1912- 2. First ladies.
3. Environmental protection. 4. Roadside improvement. 5. Urban beautification.
6. Wild flowers. 7. Women — Biography.] I. Hein, Joy Fisher, ill. II. Title.
E848.J64 A67 2005   973.923'092—dc21   2002151791

Typography by Carla Weise
1 2 3 4 5 6 7 8 9 10
❖
First Edition

ACKNOWLEDGMENTS

I want to thank Dr. Philip Scott, archivist at the Lyndon Baines Johnson Library; Mrs. Betty Tilson, assistant to Mrs. Johnson; and Shirley James, secretary to Mrs. Johnson, for their assistance during the writing of this book. My gratitude runs over to my longtime editor, Meredith Charpentier, who set this book on its course, and to Rosemary Brosnan, for bringing her loving hand to its completion.

Love, K.A.

First and foremost, my eternal gratitude to my dear friend and generous teacher, Kathi Appelt. Thank you for sharing your great talent and loving vision of Lady Bird, and for believing in my work. My best wishes to the delightful people of Karnack, Jefferson, and Uncertain, Texas, with special appreciation to Lady Margaret and True Redd for our lovely accommodations and our glorious sunset cruise on Caddo Lake. Thanks to the rangers of Caddo State Park and the staff and volunteers of the Lady Bird Johnson Wildlife Center—all of your regional flora and fauna information has been invaluable. My love and gratitude for the support of my loving husband, Frank, and my dear patient family, friends, SCBWI critique group, walking group, book group, and fellow Texas Master Naturalists.

My deepest heartfelt respect to Meredith Charpentier and Rosemary Brosnan, my wise, patient, and wonderful editors.

Always, J.F.H.

Both of us wish to thank Lady Bird Johnson and her family for the ongoing work that they do to make our world a better place.

Deep in the heart of Texas lives a woman who loves flowers. "Wildflowers," she says, "are the stuff of my heart!"

She loves the bright California poppies, the wild prairie roses in Iowa, and the thick bluebonnets of Texas, all of which grow along the highways of our great country.

There was a time when our roadsides were ugly. They were cluttered with billboards, rusted old cars, and miles of trash.

They might still be this way if not for the woman we know as Lady Bird Johnson.

She was born on December 22, 1912, in a large

mansion known as the Brick House. Her mama and

daddy, Minnie and T.J., named her Claudia Alta Taylor.

But one day her nanny held her up and declared,

"She's as purty as a lady bird." And from then on folks

called her Lady Bird, the name of the colorful and lively

beetle that grew in those parts.

The Brick House was an enchanted but lonely place for
a little girl. It stood by itself outside the village of Karnack,
surrounded by the thick pine forest of East Texas. In the
garden stood a tall magnolia tree whose enormous leaves
and huge creamy blossoms bloomed each spring. Just
beyond its grounds Lake Caddo waited, with its winding
bayous and ancient cypress trees.

Three months before Lady Bird's sixth birthday, tragedy struck. Minnie tripped at the top of the grand stairway and fell. She became seriously ill and died from blood poisoning. Lady Bird was heartbroken. Her mother had been so beautiful, so full of stories. How could she be gone?

MINNIE LEE
TAYLOR
1874–1918

Winter settled in. The trees shed their leaves, the creatures curled up in their dens, and the flowers stayed closed up tight beneath the hard red clay. The Brick House was lonelier than ever. But little Lady Bird was the loneliest of all.

One day Lady Bird heard a true story about her mama.
A neighbor told Lady Bird about an afternoon when she
saw Minnie, dressed in white, running down the drive
barefooted to meet T.J. Minnie carried a bouquet of
bluebonnets in her hand. When Lady Bird heard this
story, the scene seemed so clear to her that, when she closed
her eyes, she could see her mama holding the bouquet
of bluebonnets, her flowing white skirts brushing the
tops of her bare feet. The vision soothed Lady Bird, and
every time she saw a bluebonnet, it filled her with a sense
of being loved.

T.J. did his best to care for his young daughter. But he was a very busy man. He was the richest landholder in Harrison County. And he owned a general store where he claimed to be a "dealer in everything." On nights when he had to work late, T.J. took Lady Bird with him. When she got sleepy, he put her to bed on a cot in the upstairs room next to the coffins. Lady Bird didn't realize what they were, and her father didn't tell her, but he knew that this was no way to raise a little girl. That's when he sent for Lady Bird's Aunt Effie.

Aunt Effie was full of songs and smiles. She taught Lady
Bird how to pay attention to the wind in the pine trees and
to the way birds sing.

Aunt Effie planted daffodils in the yard at the Brick
House. When the first one bloomed each spring, Lady

Bird held a ceremony for it. She would chant, "Oh, you are so beautiful. You are the most beautiful flower in the whole world. You shall be the princess." It was as if Aunt Effie's flowers became companions and helped take some of Lady Bird's loneliness away.

Lady Bird attended a one-room schoolhouse in Karnack. She was a good student, and as she grew older she often helped her father in his general store. But not all her hours were filled with studies and work. Whenever she could, she spent her afternoons and weekends in her beloved forest. In her diary she later wrote, "I loved to paddle in those dark bayous, where time itself seemed ringed around by silence and ancient cypress trees, rich in festoons of Spanish moss. Now and then an alligator would surface like a gnarled log. It was a place of dreams."

As much as she loved the forest, though, Lady Bird yearned to explore the world beyond its tall trees, beyond the walls of the Brick House.

In 1930 it was unusual for a woman to attend college, but when Lady Bird was eighteen, she waved good-bye to T.J. and Aunt Effie and moved to Austin, where she became a student at the University of Texas. Lady Bird immediately fell in love with the rocky slopes, the brushy trees, and the wide-open sky of the hill country. And best of all, fields and fields of bluebonnets. So much was different, but the bluebonnets were the same.

The city and its surrounding hills gave her a sense of freedom that she had never felt in the pine forests of home. In a letter to a friend, she wrote, "All of the doors of the world suddenly were swung open to me."

It was a heady time for a young woman from East Texas! And it became even more so the day she met a tall, handsome fellow named Lyndon Baines Johnson. Lyndon courted Lady Bird with romantic letters that he sent almost every day. In one he wrote, "This morning I'm ambitious, proud, energetic, and very madly in love with you." Lady Bird was dazzled.

On November 17, 1934, the two were married in a small ceremony in San Antonio. For their honeymoon they traveled to Mexico, where Lady Bird marveled at the exotic flowers and trees, unlike any she had seen before. She had never been happier.

It wasn't long before Lyndon entered politics and won
a seat in the United States Congress. One of Lady Bird's
roles as the wife of a congressman was to entertain people
who came to the capital city.

Often she found herself serving as a tour guide. It was
a job she enjoyed, showing visitors the many museums and
monuments that grace Washington, D.C.

However, as she became familiar with the city, she noticed the dismal parks that were nothing more than concrete slabs, the dirty streets and shabby lawns, the unkempt and weedy shores of the filthy Potomac and Anacostia Rivers. Remembering how beautiful flowers and trees had helped her thrive, she worried about children growing up with only cement and asphalt beneath their feet.

To Lady Bird, the act of planting flowers helped people become better caretakers.

"It is important for a child to plant a seed," she told a friend, "to water it, nourish it, tend to it, watch it grow, and when he does, and when she does, they themselves will grow into great citizens."

After her two daughters, Lynda and Luci, were born, Lady Bird made sure that her garden in Washington was full of blossoms, which she planted herself, just as her Aunt Effie had done so many years before at the Brick House. But in her heart she wanted flowers for every child, not just her own.

In 1960, when John F. Kennedy was elected president of the United States, Lyndon was elected vice president. Three years later, on November 22, 1963, President Kennedy was assassinated in Dallas, Texas. On one of the most tragic days in our country's history, Lyndon became president. All at once, under the worst circumstances

imaginable, Lady Bird became the First Lady of the United States of America.

The entire country was thrown into mourning. One of Lady Bird's first responsibilities in her new position was to help her country begin to heal. In her diary she wrote, "Now the time has come to get the wheels of life rolling again."

She knew from her own experience that beauty would help the country recover. Thanks to her boundless energy, and with the urging of the president, the Highway Beautification Act was passed by Congress. Because of that law the landscapes along the interstate highways of our great land were cleared of signs and rusted cars. The roadsides were blanketed in native wildflowers.

In the capital itself, more cherry trees were planted, trees that fill the city with blossoms every spring. Best of all, a million daffodils were planted along the Potomac River, just like the ones that Lady Bird dubbed "princess" when she was a little girl.

When Lyndon's term of office ended in 1969, Lady Bird was happy to return to their home in the Texas hill country.

The ranch had suffered from years of overgrazing by the long-horned cattle that roamed its pastures. So Lady Bird gave the old place a fresh start. She planted vast fields of Texas wildflowers—Indian blankets and Indian paintbrush, bluebells, purple horsemint, and especially bluebonnets. The ranch blossomed with color and vitality.

She and Lyndon shared many happy moments driving along with their dog, Yuki, gazing in wonder at the beautiful hillsides.

But these moments were too quickly dashed. Only a few years after their return from Washington, in 1973, Lyndon's heart gave out. Lady Bird found herself mourning. Winter set in. And once again her house felt very empty.

Although she found herself alone, Lady Bird drew comfort from her old love—wildflowers. One spring afternoon, she and a friend came upon a field that was blanketed with pink evening primroses. As they stood there, Lady Bird heard the unmistakable roar of a tractor. Sure enough, from the top of the hill, a farmer appeared, mowing down the beautiful flowers. Lady Bird couldn't stand it. She climbed over the barbed-wire fence and ran toward the farmer, waving her hands. At first he ignored her, but finally she stood right in front of the tractor and he was forced to stop.

Lady Bird implored him to stop mowing, but the farmer insisted that he had to plant his hay in order to earn his living. She was about to give up when an idea struck her. "I'll pay you for your wildflower seeds," she said. She offered him enough money to make up for his losses. A deal was reached.

When she turned seventy, Lady Bird helped establish the National Wildflower Research Center. There scientists study the uses and effects of wildflowers. They also collect and preserve seeds of those flowers on the brink of extinction.

When asked why she helped found the center, Lady Bird told reporters that it was her way of "paying rent for the space I have taken up in this highly interesting world." To stand on its lovely grounds is to experience a moment of natural beauty.

Now, whenever you travel through the countryside
and you see a field of wildflowers, be sure to wave to them
as you drive by. Learn their names—the lady's slippers,
black-eyed Susans, larkspurs, winecups, blazing stars,

Granny's nightcaps. As you pass by, call out, "Thank you, Miss Lady Bird!" And remember that it hasn't always been this way. These flowers are ours to keep. They're ours to tend. They're the "stuff of our hearts."

CAN YOU FIND THESE WILDFLOWERS?

Try to find these wildflowers in the pages of this book.

(Page numbers are listed upside down below.)

BLUEBELL

BLUEBONNET

BUTTERFLY WEED

COMMON PLANTAIN

FIREWHEEL (INDIAN BLANKET)

INDIAN PAINTBRUSH

PINK EVENING PRIMROSE

PRICKLY PEAR CACTUS

PURPLE CONEFLOWER

PURPLE HORSEMINT

ROSEBAY RHODODENDRON

YELLOW AMERICAN LOTUS

Bluebell: 30, 31; Bluebonnet: 1, 3, 4, 5, 10, 11, 19, 30, 31, 32, 39; Common Plantain: 35; Butterfly Weed: 35; Firewheel: 25; Firewheel: 1, 30, 34;
Indian Paintbrush: 1, 5, 30, 32, 39; Pink Evening Primrose: 5, 19, 32, 33, 39; Prickly Pear Cactus: 19, 31; Purple Coneflower: 35;
Purple Horsemint: 31, 34; Rosebay Rhododendron: 25; Yellow American Lotus: 17

MISS LADY BIRD'S LEGACY

On December 22, 2002, Lady Bird Johnson celebrated two birthdays: her own ninetieth and the Wildflower Center's twentieth. Renamed the Lady Bird Johnson Wildflower Center, it resides on 284 acres just south of Austin, Texas. Nestled in the heart of the Texas hills, the center's mission is "to educate people about the environmental necessity, economic value, and natural beauty of native plants."

Each year thousands of schoolchildren visit the center. There they hike down the John Barr Trail, where they can see and identify wildflowers, native trees, shrubs, and cacti. The trail also features an outdoor classroom called the Persimmon, a shady spot where you can look closely at native plants and discuss the importance of caring for the landscape.

You can hike along the Savanna Meadow Trail, which includes a cave where water filters into the Edwards Aquifer. The Cedar Elm classroom along this trail has vast views of the savanna meadow. Be prepared for an explosion of colors, especially in the spring and fall.

A highlight is the Butterfly Garden, where you can observe the activities of busy butterflies, dragonflies, and other insects. There is an Insectary, a small structure that allows the center to raise butterflies in a protected, enclosed environment that is free from birds, wasps, and other predators until the butterflies are ready to fly freely. If you are lucky, a two-tailed swallowtail or a buckeye might land on your shoulder!

The Wildflower Center serves as a living laboratory. Even though it is located in Texas, its impact is nationwide. Scientists from across the country conduct research there in landscape restoration, plant conservation, horticulture, and environmental education. Mrs. Johnson has stated, "Wildflowers and native plants are as much a part of our national heritage as Old Faithful or the Capitol building." The Lady Bird Johnson Wildflower Center is not only her legacy. It's ours too.

For more information about the Lady Bird Johnson Wildflower Center or to find out what you can do to help keep our wildflowers blooming, go to www.wildflower.org.

ENDNOTES

p. 5: Martin, Ginny, producer. *Wildflowers with Helen Hayes*, video. North Texas Public Broadcasting, Inc., KERA-TV, Dallas/Ft. Worth, TX, 1992.

pp. 6–7: Flynn, Jean. *Lady: The Story of Claudia Alta (Lady Bird) Johnson*. Austin, TX: Eakin Press, 1992, p. 1.

pp. 12–13: Flynn, p. 7.

pp. 14–15: Richardson, Marlene, producer. *Lady Bird, Naturally*, video. Alamo Public Telecommunications Council, KLRN-TV, P.O. Box 9, San Antonio, TX 78291, 2001.

pp. 16–17: Middleton, Harry. *Lady Bird Johnson: A Life Well-Lived*. Austin, TX: Lyndon Baines Johnson Foundation, 1992, p. 53.

pp. 18–19: Gould, Lewis L. *Lady Bird Johnson: Our Environmental First Lady*. Lawrence: University Press of Kansas, 1999, p. 5.

pp. 20–21: Gould, p. 7.

pp. 22–23: Richardson, video.

pp. 24–25: Richardson, video.

pp. 26–27: Johnson, Mrs. Lyndon Baines. *A White House Diary*. New York: Holt, Rinehart & Winston, 1970, entry on November 26, 1963.

pp. 32–33: Richardson, video.

pp. 34–35: Flynn, p. 130.

~

SELECTED BIBLIOGRAPHY

BOOKS

Carpenter, Liz. *Ruffles and Flourishes*. New York: Pocket Books, 1971.

Flynn, Jean. *Lady: The Story of Claudia Alta (Lady Bird) Johnson*. Austin, TX: Eakin Press, 1992.

Gould, Lewis L. *Lady Bird Johnson: Our Environmental First Lady*. Lawrence: University Press of Kansas, 1999.

Johnson, Mrs. Lyndon Baines. *A White House Diary*. New York: Holt, Rinehart & Winston, 1970.

Loughmiller, Campbell & Lynn. *Texas Wildflowers: A Field Guide*. Austin: University of Texas Press, 1996.

Middleton, Harry. *Lady Bird Johnson: A Life Well-Lived*. Austin, TX: Lyndon Baines Johnson Foundation, 1992.

Wasowski, Sally and Andy. *Native Texas Plants*. Houston, TX: Gulf Publishing, 1997.

VIDEOS

Lady Bird Johnson, the Texas Wildflower. ABC News Production and A&E Television Networks, New York, 1998.

Lady Bird, Naturally. Alamo Public Telecommunications Council, KLRN-TV, San Antonio, TX, 2001.

Wildflowers with Helen Hayes. North Texas Public Broadcasting, Inc., KERA-TV, Dallas/Ft. Worth, TX, 1992.

WEBSITES

Lady Bird Johnson Wildflower Center: www.wildflower.org

Lyndon Baines Johnson Library and Museum: http://lbjlib.utexas.edu

National Gardening Association: www.kidsgardening.com